Thanks to: Paul, Rick and Bruce, for help and infinite patience; to Gill, for endless cups of coffee; to Dave, Ian and Big Kenny; to Vic Coppersmith-Heaven; to John Weller; to Paul Bradley; to Mark H.; to Angela at Polydor.

PHOTO CREDITS
Pennie Smith: Front cover, Inside back cover, pages 10, 27, 35, 40, 52, 53, 58, 60, 68, 69, 70, 71, 72, 73, 79, 83, 84 (both), 86, 90/91, 92, 95, 101, 103, 108, 110/111.
Andy Rosen: Back cover, Inside front cover, pages 64/65, 66, 75, 106/107.
Ron Cohen: pages 5, 6, 8, 30/31, 57.
Kevin Cummins: pages 11 (both), 13, 14, 18/19, 21/22, 23, 37, 43, 44, 46/47, 48, 55, 56, 98.
Doug Mckenzie: page 38.
Anton Corbijn: pages 80, 89, 105.

DISCOGRAPHY
Singles:

In The City / Takin' My Love	2058 866	29.4.77
All Around The World / Carnaby Street	2058 903	8.7.77
Modern World / Sweet Soul Music / Back In My Arms Again / Bricks And Mortar	2058 945	21.10.77
News Of The World / Aunties And Uncles / Innocent Man	2058 995	24.2.77
David Watts / A-Bomb In Wardour Street	2059 054	11.8.78
Down In The Tube Station / So Sad About Us / The Night	POSP 8	6.10.78
Strange Town / Butterfly Collector	POSP 34	9.3.79
When You're Young / Smithers-Jones	POSP 69	17.8.79
The Eton Rifles / See-Saw	POSP 83	3.10.79
Going Underground / Dreams Of Children (First 100,000 with free E.P. live versions of Down In The Tube Station / Modern World / Away From The Numbers)	POSPJ 113	7.3.80
Start! / Liza Radley	2059 266	15.8.80
Funeral Pyre / Disguises	POSP 257	29.5.81
Absolute Beginners / Tales From The Riverbank	POSP 350	16.10.81
Town Called Malice / Precious	POSP 400	29.1.82
Town Called Malice (special 12")	POSPX 400	29.1.82

Albums:

In The City	2383 447	5.1977
The Modern World	2383 475	11.1977
All Mod Cons	POLD 5008	10.1978
Setting Sons	POLD 5028	10.1979
Sound Affects	POLD 5035	11.1980
The Gift	POLD 5055	3.1982

The Jam

•

The Modern World
by Numbers

•

Paul Honeyford

Plexus, London

Published by Plexus Publishing Limited
26 Dafforne Road
London SW17 8TZ
First Printing 1995

ISBN 0 85965 219 X

A catalogue record for this book is available from the British Library.

First published in 1980 by Eel Pie Publishing Limited

Printed in Great Britain by J W Arrowsmith

10 9 8 7 6 5 4 3 2 1

START

6

Along with The Clash and the Pistols, The Jam came out of the 1976 musical earthquake known colloquially as the 'New Wave' with a determination to become not only a part of rock and roll but also to waken it from its slumbering, self-satisfied complacency. All three bands showed a vitality and urgency which is now just well-documented history, but whereas the Pistols unsurprisingly burned themselves out and The Clash allowed themselves to be thwarted by the inadequacies of the music business, The Jam forced them-selves ever onwards, screwing up as regularly as their contem-poraries but learning their lessons, adapting and refining their approach until they became, quite simply, unstoppable.

It would, however, be flippant to describe The Jam as 'the best rock and roll band in the world'. You need as many words as the Eskimoes have to describe snow to define the many different tex-tures of the rock and roll world–but Foxton, Buckler and Weller have always kept fighting hard enough to not only remain in contention for the title but also to fight the battle on their own terms. Once they had succeeded in breaking away from the naivety of the early punk explosion, they took a faded and tattered rock and roll and re-wove it into a patchwork of passion and creativity.

The early punk detonation that took place in 1976, and which threw the whole notion of rock and roll as techno-indulgence out of the proverbial window (however temporarily) was reminiscent not only of the prairie-fire growth of rock bands in 1963/64, but also of the moment in 1955 when Presley first shook his hips and sent a nation crazy. It was a return to the basics of rock and roll–emotion, aggression and commitment, a situation which has kids fighting desperately when they don't even know what they are fighting for.

The '70's had never really produced anyone who could fulfil the sacrosanct role 'spokesman for a generation', but finally the kids got tired of Dylan's platitudes, Townshend's self-imposed martyrdom and Lennon's seclusion and they demanded a new leader. Johnny Rotten threatened to be that leader–indeed, proved himself to be the self-styled führer of punk–but ultimately he failed to deliver the goods. That left Weller and Strummer as the only two serious contenders for the position, but as it turned out, The Clash did not have a wide enough appeal for Joe to succeed to the role, and rock and roll found itself trapped and inhibited by its own inbuilt weaknesses. Weller was too brash, too inconsistent at first to be anything more than a guitar with a big mouth, but he learned his lessons and he learned them fast, and with Foxton and Buckler prepared to play supporting roles without being self-deprecating about the whole thing, The Jam were at Warp Factor One and ready to fly.

IN THE FIRST PLACE...

The history of The Jam as a band can be traced back to a point some four years prior to the New Wave when Paul Weller, then attending Woking's Sheerwater Secondary Modern School, met up with Steve Brooks, who proved to have as great an inclination towards a star-spangled musical career as Paul himself. The two found themselves eminently compatible in musical tastes and general attitudes–both of them growing long hair and smoking dope to rebel like the other kids–and they formed a simple acoustic duo which they hoped would bring them much fame and fortune and an endless supply of willing teenage girls. Thus inclined, they began their search for gigs at which they might exhibit their musical prowess, and the first platform they discovered for their talents was at Woking Working Men's Club–a gig arranged, incidentally, by Paul's dad, John Weller, at that time a bricklayer.

On a fateful day in 1972, Weller and Brooks presented their first captive audience with a set which was, to say the least, not ecstatically received. Woking's working population did not appear to be stirred by the performance of Weller's self-penned ballads but, quite undismayed, the two would-be rock and roll stars decided to jettison the Simon and Garfunkel approach and began a search for another guitarist and drummer.

It wasn't until some months later, having discovered an apparent dearth of musicians in Woking, that the next link in the chain was forged when Dave Waller arrived at Sheerwater Secondary Modern. The somewhat bedraggled poet quickly endeared himself to Weller and Brooks, and Paul persuaded Waller to buy an £18 guitar and join the band. The latter obliged, but his influence on the group soon proved to be more inspirational than musical, the demon weed and Yer Blues being but two of the wonders to be introduced to the band. Nonetheless, music was not entirely forsaken and the three of them began to work on a motley collection of songs.

9

Paul swapped his Beatles souvenir guitar for bass guitar duties while Brooks and Waller played twin lead guitars, but the group still lacked a drummer.

It was at this point in time that Paul Richard Buckler arrived on the scene. Rick was some three years older than the other guys in the band and his only other musical experience was in a group he had formed with his twin brother Pete on bass. That particular group had never actually performed any gigs, the Bucklers preferring the time-honoured tradition of rehearsing in bedrooms and garages to the smell of the greasepaint and the lure of the crowd, but Rick decided to risk all and joined forces with Paul, Dave and Steve. After hauling him into the band, and christening him 'Pube' in the process, for reasons best left undisclosed, the band now found themselves with enough musicians to at least look as if they knew what they were doing, and as such they had to choose a name for themselves–a name which, of course, turned out to be The Jam, Paul having been blessed with inspiration over breakfast one morning.

Having now attained a recognisable identity, the band rehearsed diligently and prepared for live exposure. The first gig they performed as The Jam was played to some thirty or forty people, mostly loyal school friends, but things didn't quite live up to their expectations. A lack of intimacy with their chosen instruments left the band lost in no man's land, somewhere between hopeless and helpless, but despite the fact that they went down like the proverbial lead balloon they determined to continue on their way. They decided that the shortest route to instant stardom was to enter a local talent contest, the finals of which were to be held in the nearby Kingsfield social club. Intensive rehearsal schedules were drawn up, although not always adhered to, until finally the fateful day arrived. In a state of some inebriation, our four heroes proceeded to deliver the goods with a feisty version of the old chestnut *Reelin' an' Rockin* and then retired to the bar to wait anxiously for the results. Needless to say, as in all good fairy stories The Jam took first prize and were presented with the first of their rock and roll trophies, a small silver cup which Paul eagerly accepted, figuring he could either use it as an ashtray or pawn it at some future date should things get rough.

10

Now absolutely certain that rock and roll stardom was theirs for the asking, the four lads continued to rehearse until one day Dave Waller decided that poetry was better than music and, by mutual agreement, left the band to go his own way. Once again The Jam were down to a threesome and they were forced to go in search of another musician.

In mid-1974, Bruce Foxton arrived. He was the same age as Rick, having in fact gone to school with him, and up until that time had been playing in a local band called RITA—which incidentally, also included Steve Prudence who went on to play bass in The Jags. That particular band had been little more than a rehearsal group, playing only two gigs in as many years, and the pronounced lack of action caused Bruce to look for fresh horizons. To begin with, he played rhythm guitar in The Jam, but after six months' hard practice on the social club circuit in Woking, Steve Brooks left the band to open a music shop and Paul swapped instrumental duties with Bruce.

The band had now achieved its most secure and stable format, and with the added advantage of John Weller as manager, The Jam began to extend their gig circuit further into Surrey and beyond.

Most of those early gigs were arranged by John and right from the start the part he has played in relation to the band has been an unusual and interesting one. In conversations he will often talk of 'we' or even 'I' instead of 'the band' and this is indicative of how much he is, in effect, the un-named fourth member of The Jam. Paul, Rick and Bruce have always regarded him as such, and it's because

of this attitude that they developed a cohesiveness which is quite remarkable in the music business, something which has been a source of great envy to other bands. John is left to handle all the financial and business affairs and the absolute trust that the band have in him and his judgement has given them a native strength and the kind of firm foundation that others often lack. To put it simply, John won't screw the band, and in the early days he carried out a tremendous amount of work on their behalf, pushing for gigs, encouraging the various members when things were down and, to a great extent, acting as a tempering and sobering influence. Whereas Paul, Rick and Bruce all expected that rock and roll stardom would come overnight, John was acutely aware of the fact that before anything could happen they'd have to put in a few years' hard graft. He pushed the band harder and harder, cajoling them to strive constantly for improvement and stressing continuously the idea that if you've got enough belief in yourself then you *can* succeed.

It was largely John's influence that kept The Jam heading forwards rather than in ever-decreasing circles at this time. In the period before the New Wave, they were a somewhat directionless band, having even flirted with a teeny-bopper image in the early days, but John's presence gave them a focus, a channel through which they could express themselves and achieve their ultimate ambitions. As such they eventually found themselves in the right place at the right time, and because of John's help in achieving this, all three members of the band trust him implicitly.

STEPPING STONES

14

1976 proved to be the watershed year for the band–the year in which they extended their gig circuit beyond the limiting confines of Woking and its surrounding areas. The resurgence of rock and roll that took place that year, and the accompanying swell of interest on the part of small club owners and managers, led The Jam to play their first gig in London at the renowned 100 club. At that time the band were nothing more than just another rock and roll group, but the flare-up of punk and the access it afforded up and coming bands to the elitist music industry provided them with the necessary fillip to prove themselves something special.

The eruption of the New Wave, with its brash, but ultimately unfulfilled, threat to sweep away all and sundry and start anew, was inevitable. It was the logical step for music to take, to move from the seventies into the eighties, and The Jam were determined to grab their share of the action. Nonetheless, they were perceptive enough (and again John Weller's inevitable influence can be detected) to avoid simply jumping on the bandwagon. From the very early days they drew a line between themselves and the other punk protagonists, distancing themselves from the event and yet following the lead that the Pistols had supplied. They used it as a means to a specific end, as a focus for their ambition. Weller himself described the band as 'the black sheep of the New Wave' and their intentional separation from certain aspects of punk was discernible from the very beginning.

They were all aware of the fact that punk, by its very nature, would prove to be a merely temporary, and ultimately stagnant, phenomenon; they knew it could only be used as a spring-board for their ambitions, since to associate with it too closely would be suicidal. Symbolic of the band's approach was the way in which they split from The Clash's notorious White Riot tour, and ultimately, of course, their approach proved to be the right one; the self-destructive

15

attitude towards music that the early punk bands so fashionably adopted turned out to be the source of their own downfall. To champion attitude above technical proficiency is fine to begin with, but to condemn musical proficiency as redundant is really quite ludicrous. The Jam resolutely refused to adopt such an attitude, but the fact that they chose to set themselves aside from their contemporaries did not entail them distancing themselves from their audience. The situation which had existed before 1976, with ponderous techno-rock dinosaurs presenting music which was largely irrelevant to real life was something which The Jam found particularly repellent.

Rock and roll is essentially communicative in nature and intention; it's a means by which barriers are overcome and differences transcended, and from the beginning The Jam wanted to convey to their audience a sense of community. In its purest form rock and roll has always had a preoccupation with loneliness and estrangement–that's real life, and rock and roll is meant to reflect real life–but what The Jam wanted to do, perhaps more than any other band, was to create a sense of solidarity and togetherness amongst people in general and kids in particular. Weller, Foxton and Buckler wanted to construct their own youth culture, using Weller's songs not only as a means of communication but also as the very weapons with which prejudices and enforced divisions could be broken down. There was a desire within the band to prove not only that kids could play great rock and roll, but also that they could articulate valid and important sentiments in other ways, and it was this desire–a desire which burns as powerfully in Weller as it did in Townshend–which gave The Jam their initial energy, their hunger for affirmation and recognition.

The most apparent difference between The Jam and the other punk bands, however, was their idiosyncratic visual image. It's often been described as a mod image when it was, in fact, a sixties image, and there's a subtle rather than pedantic difference between the two. Paul Weller has always been into esoterica of the period 1964 to 1969 –a point perhaps best illustrated by his remark that Townshend never wrote a worthwhile lick after *Tommy*. Weller didn't simply wear '60's fashions because he liked them; it was also because he was interested in the '60's lifestyle as a whole.

His passion for that period was a rediscovery for him of something vibrant and fertile, and he took up the styles and ideas of the

16

time because 'they reeked of youth simply to look at them.' It was an approach that Foxton and Buckler quickly picked up on, and the clothes served to reinforce the visual impact of their music. Weller himself has said that the first guitar he bought was a Rickenbacker 'because it looked good.' The Jam wanted to present an image of a time of supposed glamour, a time which the vast majority of their audience was too young to remember. It wasn't simply an exercise in nostalgia, however, but rather a determined recollection and re-association with a culture which the band felt was still alive and still worthwhile. Old mods did undoubtedly check them out, perhaps initially considering them pretenders to a throne long since vacated, but the greatest percentage of their audience was unquestionably of the punk persuasion.

What The Jam were doing was adopting a culture which was unashamedly and self-consciously aesthetic in nature, but their projection of that period retained the '70's punk element of finding pleasure in real life. The '60's era has always had an inviting sense of idealism about it, and Weller the idealist wanted to reawaken the feeling that things *can* be better and that true happiness is more than just a myth.

The Jam's attempt to fuse that earlier idealism with the New Wave consciousness can perhaps best be understood when placed in context with their growing interest in Pop Art. That particular art form sought to make people aware of the intrinsic aesthetic qualities of everyday objects and situations, and that was precisely what The Jam wanted to do with their music.

The neatly styled haircuts and mohair suits straight out of Carnaby Street contrasted sharply with the torn T-shirts and garbage can liners that were high on the 1976 punk fashion lists (and, it should be noted, also high on the 1977 Paris fashion lists). On the surface The Jam, like The Beatles before them, appeared to be 'such nice boys' but whilst they were brash and as cockily self-assured as any of their contemporaries–Weller's amp used to boast the motif 'Fire and Skill'–they also avoided slipping into the hip rejection of their predecessors' music that Rotten and Co. fell into. For example, one of Paul Weller's earliest heroes was Otis Redding–at one stage he even tried to sing like him–and whilst natural ability and the desire for self-expression triumphed over hero worship in the end, the band retained a deep respect for their musical ancestry.

18

19

When Paul Weller talks, if not reverentially, at least respectfully of how *Revolver* is a great album, it brings to mind how Glen Matlock was sacked from the Pistols because 'he was into The Beatles'. The Jam's refusal to deny their allegiance and inspirational debt to The Who, The Beatles and The Stones, etc., brought them in for a hell of a lot of criticism in the early days, and the most obvious and recurring theme was that the band had jettisoned any sense of individuality in favour of a conservative, pseudo-Whoish appearance. Weller and Foxton's on-stage acrobatics and swirling windmill arms were deemed too redolent of the early Townshend to be valid, but those early critics failed to realise that The Jam were merely drawing on their roots more openly than the other New Wave bands.

The early gigs that The Jam played in London included performances of such classics as Wilson Pickett's *Midnight Hour*, Arthur Conley's *Sweet Soul Music*, Lee Dorsey's *Ride Your Pony* and even The Who's *So Sad About Us*. Inevitably they were accused of a lack of originality, but what the band saw themselves as doing, however, was simply drawing on their '60's roots in the same way that The Beatles and their contemporaries drew their inspiration from the late '50's. What had inspired Paul Weller to play rock and roll had been listening to Otis Redding, The Who and The Beatles–so why shouldn't he draw upon his influences as they drew upon theirs? Townshend, for example, more or less stole the Kinks' *You Really Got Me* for the Who's first single. Virtually every major rock musician has at sometime re-worked older songs.

With the exception of, perhaps, Elvis Costello and Joe Strummer, most of the early New Wave musicians proved to be simply purveyors of the '60's concept 'the medium is the message'. The Jam, however, were also passionately concerned with what was being *said*. It wasn't merely the fact that 16 to 18 year old kids were playing rock and roll again that was important–although that fact was celebrated in the later *Sounds From The Street*–it was that they were at last able to say something that had been awaiting a means of expression for nearly ten years. The New Wave gave English kids the opportunity to recognise their own importance, and The Jam wanted to use that awareness to its utmost.

From those early days at the 100 Club, The Jam took a path which showed them determined to adopt what was vibrant and fertile from the '60's and fuse it to a '70's street awareness, and as

22

they didn't deny the debt they owed their predecessors they succeeded in creating for themselves a far stronger musical foundation than any of the other bands could boast. To sum up their approach to music it's fitting to refer Paul Weller's response to a U.S. journalist who asked him to explain the difference between the New Wave and rock and roll: 'There *is* no difference–it's all rock and roll, and rock and roll's for dancing and having a good time.'

That attitude, coupled with their determination to be quite simply the best in the field, drove The Jam to greater and greater heights. The fact that they realised before any of their contemporaries that music is music, full stop, gave the band a head start that they haven't failed to capitalise on.

Live, The Jam quickly proved themselves to be a powerfully cohesive unit. Foxton's pulverising bass lines and Buckler's precise and intelligent drumming held together Weller's at times undisciplined chordings and provided a rock steady soap-box from which he could shout his message out loud. His frenzied image often contrasted sharply with the calmer features of Foxton and Buckler, but it was precisely that frenzy, that almost demonic aggression, that fuelled The Jam's motors.

The band had an essential power, born of an absolute conviction in their ability, and all their talents and energies were channelled into the presentation of the music. Paul Weller quickly proved himself very much the exorcist, flashing his Rickenbacker like a crucifix to rid rock and roll of its faded devils. Then again, Foxton and Buckler showed themselves to be more than simply passengers trailing in his wake. They gave his fevered articulations a powered thrust which he quite simply could not have done without, and the band as a *unit* really began to function.

Right from the start it could be seen that they put music first–at one point they even burned a copy of the fanzine 'Sniffin' Glue' on stage because it said they spent too much time tuning-up at gigs. The Jam were after quality as well as power and aggression.

BUSINESS AFFAIRS

The arrival of The Jam did not pass entirely unnoticed by those in power. In the midst of record company eagerness to sign up any band under twenty-five with a New Wave sounding name, and a flurry of A and R men with open cheques scrabbling with one another, The Jam sudenly found themselves with a record deal. Chris Parry, who later went to set up Fiction Records, signed the band to a five album deal with Polydor.

To be truthful, it was a little too early in the band's career for them to deal with the responsibilities of a recording deal comfortably –they were still raw and at times incomplete in their performance– but, abruptly finding themselves in a position of apparent security, the time had come to prove themselves. They were now part of the music business which had failed for so long to provide the kids with anything worthwhile, and their brash self-confidence was laid on the line.

What gave the band a distinct edge was that they realised that punk wasn't really a revolution in the sense of the destruction of rock and roll. The Jam simply wanted to squeeze rock's faded heroes far enough to one side for them to make their own statement– to give the kids a choice, in other words, and to do that they had to produce something notable.

Their first waxing was the single *In The City*, a relatively minor hit which nonetheless has been one of the finest they've produced. It was an intensely likeable number, and one of its greatest strengths was Foxton's inescapably catchy bass line, its melody providing a suitable backdrop for Weller's hoarse vocals. Although basic in construction, the song was perfect for the time itself, and it summed up the band's approach completely. Simplicity was coupled with power and perception to produce very good rock and roll.

The band were as essential a teenage band as any of the others around at the time, and they succeeded in articulating their frustrations in a very real and highly commercial manner. That first single was uncompromising and yet at the same time instantly saleable, and even taking into account the conditions prevailing at that time, very few bands have been as successful as The Jam in mixing the two. Perhaps the most notable exception has been Elvis Costello, who has similarly fused artistic credibility with popular appeal, but aside from him there aren't that many artists that have come out of the New Wave and sustained as consistently high a level of commerciality and quality as The Jam.

Back in 1976, the band found that first single met with reasonable if not effervescent approval, and the world awaited further developments. What the world got was The Jam's first album, also called *In The City,* and although it was phrased as a celebration of rock and roll, it was also *as a whole* a definitive teenage anthem before the term became a cliché. It contained a collection of songs that expressed a wide variety of feelings and emotions, from downright anger to the pain of unfulfilled romance, and in that respect it was very true to life. The songs hit several distinctly different targets and as such they went beyond the often one-dimensional appeal of, for example, the Pistols.

The band also chose to include two early '60's standards on the album–Larry William's *Slow Down* and the Batman theme, a track The Who performed on the *Ready, Steady, Who* E.P. As such, it reiterated the fact that they were not prepared to give up their musical heritage, but it also, of course, led to more accusations of plagiarism, and in some unkind quarters the album was described as being merely a retread of The Who's *My Generation* L.P. Admittedly, there was a similarity, particularly in some distinctly Townshendian chord progressions, but again, to say the band were influenced by The Who is like saying John Lennon was influenced by Gene Vincent and Chuck Berry. It's inevitable, and the inclusion of the two '60's songs on the album was meant as an acknowledgement of that fact.

In many respects, *In The City* contented itself with attacking conventional targets, but it also revealed a profound awareness on the part of the band as to what the New Wave was all about–or at least, what it *should* have been all about.

At the time of its release (mid 1977) all the young bands were concerned with putting out records that denigrated mainstream rock and roll attitudes, but compared to the offerings of so many of their

27

contemporaries, The Jam's efforts were potentially more constructive and optimistic in tone. Like The Clash they realised that there would be no more Elvis, Beatles and Rolling Stones, and Weller and company wanted to replace them with something that was just as dynamic, but above all, something that was far more relevant to real life. They wanted to knock down the bastions of the establishment, for sure, but they also wanted to build anew.

Rock and roll is essentially a young man's pastime; an attempt to express feelings of frustration and desperation and it is the drive to understand those feelings that gives rock and roll its basic power. Paradoxically, when that understanding is finally gained, the music loses much of its validity, but what makes the *great* rock and roll bands so good is that they constantly seek fresh goals. It's when that drive fails that the music becomes redundant.

This is a fact of life that The Jam have always appreciated and they put their knowledge to good use on that first album. It would be a terrible cliché to simply say that they were rebelling through their songs, and what emerged from that album–a theme that has been running through their music right up to the present day–is that rebellion can so easily prove to be counter-productive. Satirize the establishment successfully and you quickly become a part of that establishment; if you don't, you simply blow a fuse and you're no longer around to rebel. In *Sounds From The Street,* a tribute to the fact that at-fucking-last kids were once again playing rock and roll for kids, Weller noted that:

'We're never gonna change a thing,
    and the situation's rapidly DE-CREAS-ING.
But what can I do, I try to be true,
    at least I'm doing something'.

And he was. He wasn't going to change the world–the only rock and roll band to have ever even remotely approached that has been The Beatles–but nevertheless he had an intense desire to do *something*. The Jam realised that there's a vast difference between simply influencing kids and actually making them do something, and the difference is even greater where the establishment is concerned, but that doesn't mean you don't try.

Again;

'The U.S.A's got the sea, yeah,
    but the British kid's got the streets'

28

It's been a long time since Britain was the land of milk and honey, and nowadays the British kid has literally nothing to look forward to except the dole, and in that context the life on the streets gains a far greater significance.

It was a situation for which The Jam desperately wanted to find the solution, but in *Time For Truth* they showed they weren't prepared to accept empty answers. 'Whatever happened to the great Empire?' Weller asks, and the criticism of Callaghan's socialism was hard and unmistakable. The Jam were not prepared to pander to any one political faction, and in that respect they showed a profound awareness of the danger of trends. Left and Right are meaningless words that mask a hunger for power, and ultimately they don't really matter; if you stand on one side then everyone on the other side is an enemy, and that's divisive. The message that The Jam wanted to convey was cohesion rather than division, although in many respects Weller's songs chronicled the inevitability of the latter.

In the light of that, it can be seen that the first album was really a statement of confusion and Weller's songs were saying: 'I don't really know what I want, and until I do I'm not prepared to commit myself.' It's a sentiment expressed most clearly on the track *Changin' My Address*. Taking the classic rock and roll situation of boy/girl relationship it said:

'No one's gonna tie me down, no one's gonna tell me what to do,
Can't you see I've got to be free'

It wasn't a matter of running away from responsibilities, more a question of saying that until you realise what responsibility means, you shouldn't just blindly accept it, and it perhaps revealed a maturity in Weller's writing that many people failed to appreciate. Kids are traditionally cast in the role of young upstarts who think they know it all, but The Jam were saying quite the opposite. In *I Got By In Time* Weller sings, almost plaintively,

'I was young this is serious,
    to me she was the world,
I thought I'd never live without her,
    but I got by in time,
I suppose what you say,
    what you do don't mean nothin' at all,
I don't mean to fail anyone,
    but you know it's something that I do'

30

How many of the other New Wave bands were doing that–admitting to the fallibilities of the very culture to which they belonged? It was as deep an understanding of human nature as any psychiatrist could give, and what The Jam were saying was that they knew damn well that their views and beliefs might change, might prove themselves wrong and obsolete, and because of that they didn't intend to thrust them down anyone's throat. It was an attitude that gave the band a deep respect for the opinions of others, even though they might not particularly agree with them.

I Got By In Time was also interesting because it contained the first seeds of a theme that was to recur constantly throughout the band's music, finding its fullest expression on the *Setting Sons* album. It dealt with the inevitability of estrangement and claustrophobia that is imposed upon the individual by the passage of time, but concluded that, despite it all, life goes on. Then again, despite all this profundity, the band weren't above saying simply that 'The kids know where it's at', apparently contradicting much of what they'd said before. This is the essential nature of the album: it's one of an almost schizophrenic uncertainty and confusion, but out of it all there came a great desire for knowledge.

The simplicity of expression coupled with the mixture of perception and accessibility showed The Jam's passionate desire for communication above all else. Where so many others sought to confuse in order to impress, The Jam sought interaction, to convey their message and make their statements as simply as possible without losing quality. The album's title track had Weller singing:

> '*I wanna say, I wanna tell you,*
> *about the young idea,*
> *And if it don't work at least we tried*,'

Communication and ideals are very much flip sides of the same coin for The Jam. You can write a good rock song, with well crafted lyrics and music, but without the right attitude, without the passion and the dream, it doesn't mean a thing–and meaning and understanding are precisely what The Jam are constantly searching for.

Then again, messages mean nothing out of context. If you're going to use rock and roll as a platform, then you can't neglect the basics. First and foremost it's got to be danceable–if it isn't you fall into the trap of empty ideology–and the inclusion of *Non-Stop Dancin'* on the album was meant as a proclamation of this fact.

> *'But when you've been dancing all night long,*
> *It gives you the feeling that you belong'*

Again the community aspect is emphasised, but it's worth noting that it only gives you a feeling of solidarity. The Jam knew, even at that early stage, that you can never build a genuine rock and roll society. All you can hope for is a group within a group, a sub-culture in which kids get together and feel part of something real and worthwhile.

Non-Stop Dancin' was in fact inspired by the Wigan Soul Scene which came to everyone's notice in the early '70's. It was a phenomenon which invigorated Weller in particular–the idea of literally thousands of kids adopting and re-shaping a culture that gave them a reason to be alive–but the one drawback was that it was too localised, too esoteric to function on any national scale. Weller drew inspiration from its existence and he idealistically wanted to extend its influence further. He wanted kids from Glasgow to London, from Carlisle to Penzance, to come together and create a cohesive society of their own, an inter-related network of ideas and perceptions that would allow them to feel a part of a greater whole– and he wanted to do that through The Jam.

And yet, the band's explicit denial of any place in rock and roll for political ideologies seemed to be turned on its head by the inclusion of *Bricks And Mortar*. A more passionate denunciation of a capitalist, growth obsessed society would be hard to find, and that passion arose out of the fact that the band had personally experienced the injustices they were singing about. Weller has described Woking as being 'like a fucking bomb site', and when he sings:

> *'While hundreds are homeless,*
> *they're constructing a parking space'*

there can be no thinking, feeling human being who would disagree with the sentiments he's expressing. It's a mournful cry, bemoaning the fact that 'this is progress, nothing stands in its path' but it's also a cry of helplessness. The undoubted suffering that The Jam could see all around them, and their empathic appreciation of that suffering, only intensified the despair they felt at not being in a position to help out.

That despair manifested itself in the early days as raw aggression, a violence which often exploded through the songs like a terrorist incendiary device, but ultimately it did nothing practical. The Jam weren't actually building houses for those homeless people, and they knew it.

Those early songs were intended to bring about a growing awareness and recognition in people that the world wasn't right, and in that respect they were undoubtedly very idealistic–but were they political? The band would deny it, since the sentiments they were expressing were feelings that went beyond mere political doctrine. It was simply an expression of humanity, of solidarity and the need to grow in the face of adversity–although their intentions weren't perhaps that clearly defined in their own minds. To a great extent they were acting on an unconscious belief that things were wrong and that something should be done–and it was precisely because they didn't know what the fuck it was they should be doing that frustration took over, and at times the songs appeared disjointed and inarticulate.

The Jam didn't want to preach, but they also didn't want to sit back and pretend that things were fine; Weller's songs sought to outline problems and their possible solutions–at the same time leaving everyone to make up their own minds. Perhaps today they've reached such a high standard of musical proficiency that the problems and cracks are successfully papered over, but the dichotomy still remains–how to inform without preaching.

On that first album, the band struggled through a no man's land where brash self-confidence was mixed with uncertainty, and belief confronted with a self-questioning approach that at the time weakened their impact, but which ultimately proved to be one of their major saving graces. Everything was being questioned, even the questions themselves, and the band set themselves up as crusaders against an enemy they didn't really understand. The first rule of warfare is to know your enemy, and whereas The Jam were trying to understand what it was they wanted to change, most of the other New Wave bands were absorbed into the musical establishment before they knew what was happening.

34

In retrospect, *In The City* stands as a classic example of the confusion of ambitions which left the New Wave vulnerable and lacking a specific identity of its own. It revealed not only the confusion of the time, but also the fear that was running through the movement as a whole, a fear which left the fragile idealism of the early days open and vulnerable.

The themes which were brought into focus on the album were those which expressed the usual New Wave sentiments – violence, the city, the need to escape and good old teen rebellion – but it also contained the song which proved to be Paul Weller's personal statement of intent – *Away From The Numbers*.

That particular track, unlike, for example, *My Generation*, wasn't really a principle for a movement, but rather an individual assertion that Weller was going to search beyond the limiting confines of life as it appeared. Powerfully, yet sadly, he criticised those people who never seek to break away and then moan 'How they never had the chance to make good.' He was saying that what's wrong is that people *won't make the choice*. But listening to *Away From The Numbers*, it seems that his desire to break free of conventional lifestyles wasn't based on the belief that the world owed him a living – far from it. It was rather a declaration that he had something vital to offer, something which burned deep inside of him and which sought expression; indeed, it's something that Weller believes burns inside every human being but which too many people allow to be crushed by society. He wanted to break out of the sham security of everyday existence in which people are fed with just enough to keep them satisfied, to curtail their ambition so that they don't rebel. In *Brave New World*, Huxley's characters are given Soma to anaesthetise their individuality, but our society is more insidious. People are raised in an atmosphere where expectations and aspirations are actively discouraged, and they are guided towards specific roles in which they're made to feel sufficiently secure, and afraid to strive for change and improvement.

This is what Weller was picking up on, obviously concentrating on the kids in the early days, but as later albums were to reveal he did have a deep awareness that *all* people are in the same predicament. It was something that he himself determined to avoid, but he also didn't want to become trapped in the role of rock star, an object of adulation or sycophancy – that would have been nothing more than

36

an affirmation of the class system that we was to grow to despise.

He was determined to carry out his search in as full a manner as possible but he held no illusions about the situation. You can't denounce others without making some kind of effort yourself – and that was why, from the very beginning, The Jam were determined to be the best.

That determination might have been reflected, to some extent, in the attitudes of other bands at the time, but where The Jam differed from The Pistols etc, was in the fact that they really *did* want the opportunity of finding something new:

'I'm sick and tired of my little niche,
I'm gonna break away
        and find out what life really is'

40

THE MODERN WORLD...
AND BEYOND

Despite the admirable effort and intentions displayed on that first album, it was really nothing more than an average rock and roll record, although it did avoid the pitfall of confining the band to any specific musical label. The punk element of 'play it loud, play it fast' was obviously present, but there were other influences too.

At that time, the band had a great admiration for Dr. Feelgood –indeed, Paul Weller cites Wilko Johnson as the first '70's guitarist to really influence him–and the touches of R 'n B in the music were unmistakable. Even Weller's singing was at times reminiscent of Lee Brilleaux's harsh phrasing, and taken as a whole the album was a fine mixture of many varied styles.

Their determination to avoid the inevitable self-destruction that punk was bringing down upon itself, and the demarcation line that they drew between themselves and their contemporaries was never more apparent than on the White Riot tour of 1977. The original package of The Clash, The Jam, Subway Sect and others set off with good intentions but soon found itself prey to various tensions and frustrations that came to a head with The Jam breaking away from the tour. Although the band are reluctant to point fingers, there were various elements which contributed to the split.

Not least of these was the financial side of it all. The Jam were being paid £100 a night, out of which they had to pay for hire of P.A. and road expenses and, according to The Clash's manager at the time, were also expected to subsidise the bands lower down on the bill. In purely practical terms, an arrangement like that just wasn't on, but there were deeper differences.

It was about this time that Weller came out with his statement that 'I think we'll all vote Tory at the next election' and The Clash responded with a telegram telling The Jam that 'Maggie wants you all round for target practice tonight.' To say the least, such a situation isn't likely to encourage harmony or compatibility, but it did raise a very important point.

41

The Clash's response, however well-intentioned, was misguided; Weller wasn't making a serious political statement about the Conservatives–he's as aware as anyone that rock and roll, by definition, is anti-fascist. He simply realised that things were becoming far too hip in 1977. It was getting fashionable to be left wing, to spout socialist policies like reciting the Lord's Prayer at school assembly, and it was precisely that which Weller was kicking against. He wasn't urging the kids to vote Tory (although he keeps his politics firmly in the background, he's undoubtedly more left than right); he was simply urging them to think for themselves. In the same way that he didn't want blind acceptance of The Jam he didn't want the kids unthinkingly to accept hip doctrines spouted by anyone else–and if the price for making that point was to alienate themselves from The Clash or the New Wave as a whole, then so be it.

The band responded to the situation with the highly charged single *All Around The World*, which seemed to sum up their vision of rock and roll.

> '*All over the country, want a new direction*
> *I said all over this land, want a new reaction*'

They wanted change as much as the Pistols and The Clash wanted it, but unlike the hip anarchy that they espoused, The Jam sought a more positive solution.

> '*What's the point in saying destroy,*
> *Want a new life for everyone*'

Again it was idealistic, but it did avoid the suicidal alternatives of the other punk bands–they knew that the inevitable consequence of preaching destruction is that one day you're going to have to destroy yourself.

The band's disassociation from punk caused their rivals to join with the rest of their critics in condemning their supposedly imitatory approach, and it was largely in response to this short-sighted criticism that Weller wrote *(This Is) The Modern World*–a song whose title was to become a by-word for the following year and beyond. Its inspiration came largely from an attempt to get back at those people who were trying to lumber The Jam with a revivalist tag, and as Weller says about the song, 'We were just trying to say that we're a new band with new ideas and things to say.'

It was an important point to make, since at this time the criticisms were coming thick and fast, with the band constantly being referred to in a derogatory fashion as 'the new Who'. When Weller is asked about the comparisons, his response is typically honest and lucid: 'It's not something I could really dispute. I *was* trying to copy Townshend. I fucking idolised him – I like the way he moves on stage and therefore it was quite natural I should want to be like that.'

But what The Jam *were* unhappy about, and the point they were trying to make, was that it was quite ridiculous to stigmatise the band as one which was only re-hashing old ideas and themes.

With that third single, in a blistering, three-minute performance, The Jam stated precisely how the Modern World demanded from

44

them not only commitment, but also an aggression which often bordered on the pompous. Their self-assurance and determination to be the greatest was unequivocal:

> 'Even at school I felt quite sure,
>   that one day I would be on top,
> And look down upon the map,
>   of teachers who said I'd be nothing'.

The band wanted recognition and praise, but it had to be deserved and not simply adulatory. They could still remember how sycophantic rock and roll had become in the early '70's and, they didn't want to become comic-book heroes. They made it quite clear that it was the kids that mattered, not the critics.

> 'Don't have to explain myself to you,
> Don't give two fucks about your review'

That 'fuck' was in fact replaced with 'damn' on the single and it was the band's first overt compromise. What it signified, however, was not a slip into the rut of commercialism but a desire for access, a cause which has always been close to the band's collective heart. To put it simply, the kids listen to the radio and neither the B.B.C. nor the independent radio stations play songs with 'fuck' in them.

As a result, they found themselves with the dubious honour of performing the song on Top of the Pops, a performance which must rank with the video of the Pistol's *Pretty Vacant* as one of the high spots of the decade. Weller's searing guitar pyrotechnics and Foxton and Buckler's thundering rhythm burned holes in everybody's ears, raising Top of the Pops from its usual morass of mediocrity.

The various merits and demerits of that particular programme have been aired often enough to need no re-iteration here, but the reason The Jam choose to perform on it are two-fold. Obviously it sells more records, and The Jam have never denied that they want success, but it also means greater access to the kids. 'People can see us when we're not touring. Kids up in Glasgow or wherever can at least have a limited form of contact with us; and that's what the band consider to be most important.

The B-side of the single contained versions of Arthur Conley's *Sweet Soul Music* and Holland-Dozier-Holland's *Back In My Arms Again* and once more it was a determined restatement of their genuine love

48

for the music of the '60's. It also reinforced the message of the A-side, since at that time it would have been very simple for them to stop playing old songs and thereby side-step the revivalist tag that so many people wanted to thrust upon them.

It was about this time that The Jam significantly reappraised their visual image for the first time. Up until then, they had made wide and pronounced use of Union Jack backdrops and badges to reinforce their presentation of the music–indeed, in the same way that The Who were responsible for all those red, white and blue artifacts of the '60's, The Jam were responsible for their resurgence. It's a little known fact, but before Townshend's Union Jack jackets of 1965 there was no use of the flag on souvenirs or decorations at all.

The band's music had already showed how they looked back upon and acknowledged a solid history, and the use of the Union Jack was meant to be an affirmation of this fact without any right-wing overtones whatsoever. It is possible to be patriotic without being fascist, the denial of which is a fundamentally insidious aspect of fascism.

The growth of the odious National Front, however, and the propaganda use they made of the Union Jack, motivated The Jam to reconsider their position, and they stopped using the motif. The associations that were being drawn between their presentation and that of the fascist organisation were cut off at the source, and although their action is understandable, on reflection it was perhaps a mistake. In so doing, the band allowed a group of right wing fools to dictate to them and, perhaps more importantly, it also made it that little bit harder to be proud of being British.

From now on, The Jam were to express patriotism through their music–most clearly on the *Setting Sons* album. But in 1977 the band were left with the need to bring out a record that would silence the critics once and for all.

After the excellent duo of *All Around The World* and *Modern World*, the eagerly awaited second album arrived–and some were disappointed. Indeed, in some quarters the album was well and truly panned, and Weller was motivated to respond that time would prove it a modern classic. It was an emotional reaction based on the fact that the band had spent a long time working on the album only to have the critics write it off in the space of five minutes. On reflection the band are willing to admit that they did succumb to various pressures at the time. They had, after all, recorded two albums, toured America, Europe and Britain twice in less than a year, but despite all that, much of that early criticism was misplaced.

The Jam were attempting to expand their horizons, to escape from the rut of simply churning out the same old stuff again and again, but that seemed to be largely ignored. It is true that the album lacked a certain cohesion, but that in itself isn't enough to explain the amount of criticism that was heaped upon it. It was an album of often disparate songs, but that's no great fault, and The Jam were quickly left with the impression that much of the criticism was rather petty. It would be fair to say that some journalists were simply playing the old game of 'set 'em up and knock 'em down again.'

However, some of the criticism was well thought out and lucidly presented. Charles Shaar Murray, for example, has been logged as saying that the band should have postponed the second album and concentrated on putting out one blistering hit single after another. It was a valid point, but the album wasn't as bad as people were making out–and besides, The Jam had no wish to become the Bee Gees of the New Wave.

The heavy critical hammering that the band received put them under severe strain and they came within shooting distance of breaking up. Fortunately, the strong family element in the band, which arose from the fact that they'd been playing together for some three years before signing to Polydor–and from John Weller's absolute commitment to their future–carried them through that particular trough. John was perhaps the most important factor in their recovery, a unifying force which refused to let them give up.

The album contained twelve tracks (although the U.S. version also included *All Around The World* and, for delicate American sensibilities, the censored version of the title track) and it proved to be the first real indication of the special relationship that Paul Weller has with The Jam. To a great extent, he constitutes fifty percent of the band–he is, after all, guitarist and principal songwriter–but it works both ways. Neither could exist without the other, but on *The Modern World* it would be fair to say that the balance was wrong. The band were beginning to stretch, and in so doing may well have over-reached themselves.

They were looking in every direction at once and some of Weller's song-writing showed a return to the ballads he'd been

50

turning out in the early days. *I Need You (For Someone)* and even *Tonight At Noon* seemed to be an attempt to transcend musical barriers, to make rock and roll romantic without being mawkish, but it didn't really work. The task is not an impossible one (The Jam succeeded on later albums), but at that time it was perhaps too difficult for the band to pull off.

Tonight At Noon was in fact inspired by two poems by Adrian Henri, the title being taken from one and the theme from another, and already Weller was beginning to extend his understanding and knowledge of '60's culture beyond its music and fashions. Adrian Henri was a member of the Liverpool poetry group which also included Roger McGough, later a founder-member of The Scaffold, and what is perhaps interesting is that it's a northern school of literature. Weller had already shown interest in the Wigan Soul Scene, and although it would be facetious to generalise about the fact, much of his inspiration does seem to come from nothern sources. One of his favourite authors is Alan Sillitoe, a Nottinghamshire lad, and one is tempted to believe that what attracted him to that area was the sense of companionship and hospitality the north is famed for. Whatever, *Tonight At Noon* was the first real indication of that interest and it was to be further developed in later material.

The album also contained various criticisms of the system as it stands–criticisms which the band were to question in the later *Saturday's Kids*–but at that time they continued to present a certain unrefined idealism to the world at large. Weller's *Standards Rule O.K.* and Bruce Foxton's *Don't Tell Them You're Sane* and *London Traffic* all dealt specifically with the facelessness of modern society. The world was seen in terms of some vast, freedom-denying institution in which everyone is inhibited and deliberately misdirected:

'The warders fill him full of lies...
Just a word out of place and he's sent to his room'

It was idealistic and naïve but it arose out of a genuine frustration that things are not as they should be, and that frustration has been one of the band's prime sources of motivation all along the line.

Then again, they've always been determined to avoid the pitfall of self-pity that such an approach might lead them into. *Here Comes The Weekend*, reminiscent in many ways of *Non-Stop Dancin'* on the first album, expressed the idea that, whatever little you've got, you just have to make the most of it:

'Everything feels right now,
    I know why I'm alive now,
Everything else is a lie now,
    Now I know why I'm here'

It was almost a statement that you can't appreciate real freedom until you've experienced restriction–again a theme to be re-examined in the later albums.

Another song on the album was, in fact, a poem written by erstwhile Jam member Dave Waller and put to music by Paul. The similarities in their approach are apparent on the first hearing, as the lyrics could easily have been written by Weller himself, and once again the theme of In The Street Today concerns the recognition of frustration without offering any concrete solution–and that is perhaps the ultimate frustration. The Jam recognise certain imperfect situations but they don't really offer any alternatives, casting themselves in the role of observers and commentators. That position is never more explicitly revealed than on Life From A Window:

'Up here I can see the world, ooh,
    sometimes it don't seem nice–that's okay
Staring at a grey sky,
    try to paint it blue–teenage blue'

There's an intimation that, despite all their efforts, nothing's ever going to really change, but they have to keep on trying.

The situations which the band were portraying all dealt to some degree with the problems of estrangement and crushed individuality and those themes were brought together most clearly on what Weller considers to be one of the best tracks on the album: The Combine–inspired primarily by One Flew Over The Cuckoo's Nest, the book by the American poet and novelist of the '60's, Ken Kesey. Society needs its rebels to appear 'democratic', a fact which Weller was quick to observe, but so many of them are impotent rebels, either kept at a safe distance or quickly taken out of circulation. The only ones in a position to profitably rebel don't want to do so any more because they've become 'establishment'. Witness The Who playing My Generation for the umpteenth time when they know damn well they don't mean it any more.

Also included on the album was Wilson Pickett's Midnight Hour, played at a thousand miles an hour and quite indecipherable, but that

54

55

seemed to sum the band up perfectly–they were impatient to move
on but as yet were unsure which direction to take.

The general lack of support for the album left the band in a
difficult situation. The pressure had been on them to produce the
goods and it appeared they hadn't. The strain was apparent and
panic threatened to set in, but their close friendship with one another
and the omnipresent figure of John Weller chivvying them along
made them determined to spring back.

57

58

NEW BEGINNINGS

The period after the second album was a time in which the whole Jam strategy underwent a drastic re-think, and some fundamental approaches were questioned. At one stage they even considered a change of producer, having up until then used Vic Coppersmith-Heaven on all of their material – who, apart from a well-attested track record, (having worked with the Stones and Cat Stevens in the '60's) had produced some of the early Clash demos. Although various alternatives were considered, none were chosen, and today the band are quite adamant that it's a damn good thing they didn't get rid of him; he works well with them, accepting advice without being acquiescent and he has a deep appreciation of rock and roll that few can equal. It's largely due to the fact that they've grown with him that the band have developed as well as they have done.

Nonetheless, 1978 opened with doubts creeping in and they became more apparent with the release of *News Of The World* in February of that year. It's been the band's only real flop and its lack of success may well have been a direct result of a surfeit of democracy in the band. Two of the tracks – the title and *Innocent Man* with its *Baba O'Riley* guitar chords – were written by Bruce Foxton. Although Bruce isn't a *bad* song-writer by any means, to a certain extent he is a less passionate and overtly idealistic character than Weller, and the aggression and commitment that had so characterised the band's earlier releases was missing. Perhaps Weller was finding it difficult to find a new direction in his song-writing and wasn't able to produce the material that was necessary, but that single did epitomise the confusion that they were feeling at the time.

It was time to seek a new identity, and the simple black and white image of mohair suits and button-down collars was left behind in the wake of the need to progress. It quickly became apparent, however, just how much the band had relied on that visual image to get them through; they were unsure of themselves and what they

60

were doing, and then to cap it all they'd been to the States to find themselves ignored by a nation anaesthetised by M.O.R. radio.

For six months they went into seclusion, letting the old Jam die down so that the new material would be judged on its own merits. In August 1978 they released the double A-side of *David Watts* and *A-bomb in Wardour Street* the former being an obscure Ray Davies song which even the Kinks mainman himself had probably forgotten he'd written–but it was given a healthy Jam production job and showed times were on the up.

What really proved that the band were back in the big league, however, was *A-bomb*, a seething re-assessment of the youth explosion that had so recently taken place. Based primarily on the *Can't Explain* riff, it was simple but highly effective, and the passion and vehemence of its message indicated that Weller had discerned the extent to which the whole punk/youth phenomenon was beginning to peter out. It wasn't so much a cry for a return to the old days, more a call to arms, a demand for those who cared to stand up and be counted once again. How many actually heeded that call is debatable, but it was really that song more than any other that showed The Jam were back on course.

It was about this time that the band abandoned much of the material from their projected third album. A complete set of songs had been recorded but the band, displaying the strict quality control that has sustained them ever since, decided that they weren't good enough. The adverse critical reactions that *The Modern World* had provoked had taught them a lesson that they weren't going to ignore.

The jettisoned album contained some ten songs, but as Weller explained: 'The songs just weren't up to standard. It was a bad period for The Jam, and a lot of the trouble stemmed from me–I was writing soppy songs or trying to be flash and arty, and I know that's not what The Jam are about. Those songs were a complete nonsense'.

Some of the tracks were re-recorded and surfaced later on– one being Bruce Foxton's song *The Night*, which turned up on the flip side of *Down In The Tube Station*. One which didn't make it was *I Want To Paint*, which Weller has described as 'more of a poem than a song'. Again he purloined the title from a poem by Adrian Henri, but the insecurity and confusion dominating the period prevented anything worthwhile coming from it. Nonetheless, it was a good idea and one which Weller feels might resurface at some later date.

Many of those songs had been written whilst the band were on tour in the States, but they nonetheless remained idiosyncratically English. The Jam had passed through the ghettos and witnessed the hate-filled racism of the South, but they didn't feel qualified to write or sing about such problems, using them rather as an inspiration to write about English problems and injustices.

That trip to the States also motivated Weller to write the haunting *English Rose*, perhaps the most deeply personal of his songs ever to be released. On one level it simply expresses his love for his girlfriend Gill, but it also describes the way he felt himself acutely separated from his own Englishness. He was caught in America, a country whose lack of intimacy doesn't exactly enthrall him, and he really wanted to be back where he felt most at home.

> 'No matter where I roam,
> I will return to my English Rose,
> For no bonds can ever keep me from she'

That song might never have been released if they hadn't redone the third album, and even then it wasn't credited on the sleeve. What it did reveal, however, was a significant step forward in the rock and roll romanticism that the band had attempted but had failed to accomplish on the second album.

Finally, in October 1978, *All Mod Cons* was released to universal critical acclaim. Some of the tracks were off the rejected album: *A-bomb, Billy Hunt* in a greatly re-shaped form, *To Be Someone* and *It's Too Bad*—and they all had something in common that the other songs lacked.

The aborted third album had been recorded with Chris Parry as engineer, but their lack of success in completing it, coupled with a determination to prove that they could still cut the ice, caused them to prune the production side of things and Chris was no longer used. The situation has been described by the band as 'simply too many cooks', and it was aggravated by the fact that they were becoming far more independently imaginative. Whereas in the early days they had taken little initiative in the production of their material, they were now beginning to adopt far more creative roles, and that was simply too much for the old scheme of things to bear. It wasn't that Chris Parry was inadequate—his later successes with Fiction Records refute that—but simply that there was one head too many and

62

someone had to go. It was perhaps that which gave the band the sort of final stimulus that they sorely needed.

All Mod Cons dealt with a vast spectrum of problems and ideas, and the determination to produce a killer album shone through. The title track showed more than any other the growing disillusionment the band was beginning to experience with the rock and roll business and the suffocating limitations it imposed upon them. It was a passionate put-down of all those hangers on who seem to breed so uncontrollably in the world of rock and roll.

That track was intended as a proclamation of the fact that the band were no longer naive Woking upstarts–they were now astute, tempered rock and rollers who held no illusions about the business to which they belonged:

'Seen you before, I know your sort...
You'll waste my time when the time comes'

To a certain extent the sentiments reflected those of *(This Is) The Modern World,* but this time around they were more clearly formulated. The message was clear–no hanger-on was going to bleed The Jam like a leech–and that message recurs constantly not only in the band's music, but also in the set-up they have behind the scenes.

From the very beginning they've taken great care to build up a hard core of loyal employees, creating a definite family unit in which they can function. All the roadies and assistants exhibit an unshakeable loyalty towards the band, and with the whole thing co-ordinated by John Weller, nothing is allowed to hang loose. Nothing is farmed out–even the band's fan club is run by Paul's sister, Nicola–and the overall impression is that in no way will anyone have the chance to screw The Jam. They have total quality control, not only in their music but also in the peripheral aspects of the business, and as such they've successfully minimised the possibility of exploitation.

But that third album wasn't just an extended put-down of the music business. *To Be Someone (Didn't We Have A Nice Time)* was a marvellously constructed scenario which dealt with everything from teenage fantasies and romanticising to a theme which was to dominate Weller's writing more and more–the essential transitoriness of life.

The first part of the song is a simple expression of every kid's dream to escape the monotony of normal existence, and the only

63

opportunity they might have to do that is to be a 'famous footballer, a rock singer or a big film star.' It's a dream that maybe one in ten thousand achieves, but without those dreams life would be almost unbearable for most kids.

Then again, it's not simply a wish to escape the so-called realities of life, rather it's a desire to gain the chance to do something worth-while. Weller appreciated that fact more acutely than most, even whilst acknowledging his own, privileged position, but what made the song special was that he knew such hopes are ultimately unful-filling. Fashions change and heroes fall and:

'The bread I spend is like my fame –
    it's quickly diminished'

The Jam were beginning to carve out their own little niche, a fact which obviously pleased them, but they knew that there was always the possibility that things would change.

66

There's an air of desperation about the song, a sense of intensely searching for something, and it is perhaps that searching aspect that has caused the band to steer clear of any overt politicising. Systems and theories may look fine on paper but ultimately they never deliver the perfect society they claim to offer.

In one of his poems, Paul Weller said: 'I've discovered that the universal language is laughter–So what's the problem?', and The Jam's frustration arises simply from the fact that no-one else seems to appreciate that. That being the case, the only thing that they can offer is to enjoy yourself whilst you can:

> 'But didn't we have a nice time,
> wasn't it such a fine time?'

It's not a defeatist attitude, however. Although possible avenues of fulfillment have turned out to be dead ends, The Jam still keep on searching, and that's more optimistic than most. *To Be Someone* once again outlined the problem without offering any specific solution, and Weller cast himself as much in the role of pupil as that of teacher.

Many of the band's later songs reveal a certain ambiguity, allowing the listener to pick up on whatever suits him or her–a quality which has been apparent in all the great song-writers from Dylan, Townshend and Lennon onwards. It seems that, the greater the freedom to make unequivocal statements, the more The Jam avoid making them.

Take as an example, *Mr. Clean*. On the surface it's nothing more than a put-down of the conventional twentieth century suburbanite, the kind of chap who meekly plays out his role in society, but beneath that veneer there lies a wealth of interests and intentions. It contained the seeds of various ideas which later came to fruition on the *Setting Sons* album, and concerned itself to a great extent with the human predicament. The 'Mr. Clean' being harangued is shown as a victim, forced to fulfill the incessant, empty demands of his role in life:

> 'Getting pissed at the annual office do,
> Smart blue suit and you went to Cambridge too'

What is interesting, however, is that it is a *middle class* existence, and the fact that it comes under Weller's scrutiny shows how directly he was beginning to concern himself with the iniquities of the class system. It's something which he finds particularly abhorrent and

70

72

perplexing: 'It's insane that something like that should exist in today's society.'

The song also shows the extent to which he feels an association with not only 'working-class' aspects of life but also anything that is unpretentious. Only the rich can afford real pretensions:

'You miss Page Three but The Times is right for you'

The Jam find the need to pretend and to function within pre-determined behaviour patterns upsetting and not a little sad, simply because it doesn't allow a person to be himself. There's a tendency in this society to work to other people's expectations, whether family, friends or bosses:

'And Mum and Dad are very proud of you'

To a great extent, The Jam are their own bosses, but even they feel that they've 'only got control of compromises.' Most people don't even have that kind of control, and yet without it how can there be the possibility of progress? The status quo is regarded as almost sacred in this society, because by maintaining it an elitist minority can keep a great number of ordinary people under control, a point clearly re-iterated on In The Crowd:

'And everyone seems that they're acting a dream,
'Cause they're just not thinking about each other,
And they're taking orders
Which are media spawned,
And they should know better,
Now you have been warned,
And life just simply moves along
In simple house, simple jobs,
And no one's wanting for the change'

That's what The Jam find so upsetting; not that people have boring, unresponding lives but that they seem quite prepared to carry on with them, scared to make a move of any kind. It's really an extension of the whole New Wave mentality, the idea of becoming so disillusioned with the established order that you get up and change it–or at least look for a viable alternative. 1976 saw the music business undergo that kind of change, and what The Jam would like too see is the same kind of process take place in life in general.

It's idealistic, but then again The Jam have always been idealists and out of all the original New Wave protagonists only they, and possibly The Clash, have come near to carrying on the ideas without stagnating. Too many of the early punk heroes gave up the struggle and slipped into their own little routines, either churning out the same old cliches or content to string along in the wake of others.

One kid once criticised Weller directly for *Mr. Clean* on the grounds that the existence described within it was the only one available to him. Weller's response was: 'Sure that's the only existence many kids have open to them, but before they listen to others and accept unresistingly, they should explore every possible avenue of escape.'

The Jam sought escape and found it, but they're nonetheless aware that thousands of other kids never even have the chance to try. All they end up with is a world of dreams and unfulfilled ambitions, a world which for *Billy Hunt* is:

> *'...a magical world,*
> *full of strippers and long-legged girls...*
> *But one day, when I get fit and grow bionic arms,*
> *the whole world's gonna wish it hadn't been born'*

The vehemence of *Away From The Numbers*, with its scornful dismissal of all those who moan that 'they never had the chance to break free', was being replaced with a real concern for the predicament of others.

It's been said that Weller allows himself to accept unjustified situations, that he's given up the struggle and become a toothless bear, occasionally roaring but primarily satisfied to shuffle around and remain detached from the whole situation. Needless to say, he's not like that, and what that third album revealed was that The Jam were extending their focus of attention to cover human problems on a far wider scale. The Beatle-ish, pure pop of *It's Too Bad* showed a concern for the breakdown of human relationships that was soon to dominate not only Weller's song material but also his whole approach to life in general.

> *'I could say I'm sorry,*
> *but that's not the point is it?*
> *You want to play your games*
> *and you don't mind if I get hurt'*

Life is shown in many respects to be a long, painful experience, involving an endless catalogue of broken relationships. There *is* an ideal world but it is glimpsed only in the distance and because of that the simple joys and pleasures of everyday situations have to be treasured that much more intensely.

This is a point re-iterated on *Fly*, a song which perhaps shows Weller at his most philosophical. It's not simply the idea of soaring away into the 'demi-monde, the twilight zone' which gives the song its searching aspect, rather it's that all the problems that Weller sees in life, and the whole question of the meaning of life in general, are seen as capable of being answered by one relationship:

> *'I see the answers, place my trust in you'.*

It shows Weller as much in the role of seeker as the early Townshend, but whereas the latter found Meher Baba, Weller's still

76

searching. Despair and cynicism at the human situation rise to the surface and:

'It seems that man cannot survive at all'

There's an apparent contradiction in *The Place I Love* and it's summed up in Weller's personal view of himself in the final verse:

'With cherished thoughts and bitterness,
I'm making a stand against the world,
There are those who would hurt us if they tried,
And that's always in the back of my mind'

It's a description of confusion, of the desire to be open and idealistic and yet finding frustration and injustice at every turn, and that's what life is for Weller–a vast potential of opportunity that is at the same time threatening and suffocating.

That threat was most powerfully portrayed on the final track of the album, *Down In The Tube Station At Midnight*. It was a masterpiece of evocative imagery and precision musicianship, and but for the fact that the B.B.C. found it disconcerting and refused even to play the damn thing, it would surely have been as successful as any of the later singles.

It was a song with a dramatic sense of realism. People seem to be in constant fear of some right wing idiot attacking them for no reason –the message seems to be that you can't even enjoy what little you've got.

It also showed that Weller had finally come to terms with the strange, illegitimate art that is rock poetry. Once again The Jam were cast in the role of commentators, observing the situation and yet remaining passionately aware of its realities and consequences. That, coupled with the surging power of the musical performance, made it a great example of what rock and roll is capable of achieving.

That third album cast Weller, in particular, in the role of the idealist, the radical, the romantic and the philosopher, but every song on *All Mod Cons* retained the essential ingredients of great rock and roll–it was infectious, it was passionate, and above all, it was danceable.

It also contained the first hint of inter-linking themes, letting the songs, as Weller says, give rise to a recurring idea, an approach that was to find its fullest exposition on the *Setting Sons* album.

And yet it wasn't only Weller's lyrical abilities that had shown marked improvement. The adeptness and imagination of Foxton and Buckler was now such an integral part of his writing that without them the material wouldn't have been half as good as it eventually proved to be. Weller's occasional tendency towards undisciplined guitar performances and stream of consciousness verse was not so much kept in check as allowed to flourish within a solid rhythmic framework that Bruce and Rick provided almost effortlessly. The ordered chaos of *A-bomb In Wardour Street* perhaps made the point clearly enough, but suffice to say *All Mod Cons* revealed that The Jam were most emphatically a cohesive, interdependent band.

SETTING STANDARDS

'We're not trendsetters and it doesn't matter that it's a revival–any movement's good that brings new ideas. It's all about new kids being into new music–and it's definitely not us that started the fashion.'

As 1978 drew to a close the resurgence of the mod movement began to consolidate itself and The Jam found themselves regarded as the heads of a youth culture for which they didn't really feel responsible. Weller personally had been into the '60's lifestyle for some five or six years and the fervency with which the music business cast them as 'mod innovators' was viewed with some disfavour. The

79

80

band have never wanted to associate themselves with any specific movement–they showed that in the way they consciously disassociated themselves from punk–and that attitude is indicative of how they want to remain as detached from the music business as possible.

'We take an interest but we don't get involved. That's why I've always said I don't feel part of the music *business*. I see us as a group the same way I did when we were fifteen and starting off. Maybe it's not entirely true, but it's how I like to look at it.'

In March 1979 they released *Strange Town*, a song which mourned the fact that the music scene was rapidly returning to what it was pre-New Wave, and that all the vitality and honesty of the early days has been lost. The kids have once again lost control and you can't deviate from the given path:

> 'You've got to walk in a straight line,
> You've got to walk and talk in four-four time'

There now seems such a distance between The Jam and the other original New Wave bands that Weller can't help but feel:

> 'I'm really a spaceman from those U.F.O.'s'

The essential unity of those early days had been lost and it was back to dog eat dog, with various bands acting out media spawned roles. All the past so-called revolutionaries were either playing the star or were setting themselves up as rock and roll martyrs, and The Jam feel that the crucial point came when all the bands finally got their recording contracts; they became rivals instead of compatriots in crime.

Strange Town in fact involved a whole new sound for the band, a determined innovation that showed them once again striving for something beyond the obvious. The four or five separate, yet musically interlocking sections within the overall structure showed that finally, and after many failures, The Jam's musical proficiency and perception matched their ambitions. Even the lethargic American public picked up on it and it was included on *Setting Sons* over there.

The B-side of that single, the haunting *Butterfly Collector*, was almost psychedelic in character and it was something of an experimental track. It was unlike anything that they'd done before, whilst retaining The Jam trademark, and the only other track which bears any similarity to it is the later *Dreams Of Children*. It showed the band more determined than ever to push onwards and avoid stagnation, to grow and develop as fully as possible regardless of any limitations that the music business might seek to impose upon them.

The band's criticism of other people for their lack of adventure becomes more acceptable in the face of their own desire for progress. For The Jam it's always been a question of intention:

'There're some bands whose music I don't like but who I admire because of their attitude–that's the most important thing. Similarly, I enjoy talking to people who are interested in what they're doing. I don't like people who are just doing their job, just interviewing so that they can collect a good wage at the end of the week. There're a lot of people who just come in, stick the tape on and it's all for money.'

Then again, The Jam no longer fall into the trap of mourning lost opportunities and repressive situations. They're not above satirizing their own intentions and those of the generation to which they belong, and the release of *When You're Young* in August 1979 was a prime example of that. On the surface, the song celebrates the joys and innocence of lost youth:

'*Life is timeless, dreams are long, when you're young,*
    you used to fall in love with everyone,
Life is a drink and you get drunk when you're young'

but The Jam's intentions went far beyond that. The song was heavily ironic, the point being that youth isn't really the Utopia that it's so often made out to be. It's a time of intense frustration, of pain and often uncontrolled anger, and yet so many people seem to glorify it.

'*Tears of rage run down your face and still you say it's fun*'

But then again, The Jam aren't simply emphasising age over youth. What they're seeking is not merely an escape from the frustrations of youth:

'*But then you find out life isn't like that,*
    and you try so hard to understand.
Why the world is your oyster
    but your future's a clam'

What The Jam want is a fusion, a mixture of the energy and idealism that so characterises youth, with the astuteness and applica-

82

84

tion that comes with age. And again, they have no time for the people who stand to one side and bemoan 'missed chances'. There's a discernible sarcasm in Weller's voice as he sings:

'But it's alright, you've got time on your side,
They're never ever gonna make you stand in line,
And you're just waiting for the right time'

Too many people have slipped into the pre-New Wave attitude of allowing themselves to feel satisfied with the situation as it stands. What The Jam want is passion, commitment and, above all, *action*.

The B-side of the single was *Smithers-Jones*, given a conventional rock and roll treatment despite the fact that on *Setting Sons* it was arranged à la Johann Strauss. It's one of Bruce's songs, and as time has passed he seems to have taken a somewhat backseat role in the song-writing department. Then again, it's not something he feels particularly envious or angry about and it'll be a long time before we see the Bruce Foxton solo album because 'if I had the bloody songs they'd be on The Jam albums'.

1979 also saw the band finally graduate to a position where they could sell out the larger rock and roll venues many times over, but it also brought with it the added concern that the communication with their audience which was so important to them was being restricted. It's an eternal rock and roll paradox–none of the band likes playing the larger venues but they need to in order to accommodate everyone who wants to see them.

In the early days, when they were playing the Woking social clubs and occasional London pubs, one of the original faithful swore that he'd never go and see them once they started playing the likes of the Hammersmith Odeon and the Rainbow, and he kept his word. He'll watch them when they occasionally play the small halls, but nothing bigger, and when the band talk about him it's clear that they feel they lost something tangible when they moved up the scale. They know that the sense of communication and common identity which pervaded all the earlier concerts has to a great extent been lost, but unlike so many other bands they haven't fallen into the trap of playing the role of distanced heroes. They've sought closer contact with people, not only through the songs but also more directly. They will often let young kids sit in on interviews, letting them chip in on occasion, and their time at the studios often resembles open-house.

Anyone and everyone who's genuinely interested is welcome, and that kind of attitude is an unfortunate rarity in today's music business.

That desire for communication and the band's deeply held antagonism towards any form of elitism has also found expression in various practical respects. For example, the launch of the Two-Tone label was something which they found particularly invigorating, in that once again young bands were gaining access to the music business whilst avoiding the tentacles of the big corporations. The Jam made a similar point of actively helping those who needed assistance. Weller worked with the late lamented and vastly under-rated Nips, whilst Foxton is co-manager with John Weller of The Vapors, a band he spotted playing in a pub in Guildford and who have since shot to the dizzy heights of fame under his guidance.

From the very beginning the band determined that, should any of them come across others they thought worthy of assistance, they would help them along, and that is precisely what they did. Weller, however, went a little further and set up his own publishing company, Riot Stories, in order to help young poets and writers.* The company's first publication was a collection of poems by erstwhile Jam member Dave Waller, and the whole operation is viewed with great optimism by Weller. He has a close affinity with literature, gaining much of his inspiration from it, and Riot Stories has allowed him the opportunity to encourage young artists in a field outside rock and roll. The fact that they can offer encouragement, and give others a chance to prove themselves and make the most of their talents is something that The Jam find very satisfying.

*For anyone interested, Riot Stories can be contacted c/o Flat 3, 1 Hyde Park Place, London W2 2LH.

90

92

THAT'S ENTERTAINMENT

Out of the turmoil of 1979 came *Setting Sons* which has been described (quite wrongly) as Paul Weller's solo album and (mistakenly) as a concept album. There can be little disagreement that it's the best album they've produced.

It was referred to in some quarters as a concept album because certain specific songs do link together, and there is a thread that runs through the album as a whole, but the band by no means intended it to be a 'concept'. The recurring militaristic image was interesting–not least because the return to uniforms was reminiscent of the black and white suits of 1976–but there's no recognisable story-line, no deaf, dumb and blind infantryman riding down to Brighton on his scooter. The themes which do show themselves to be inter-linked are all about the problems of estrangement, of the distances that develop between people.

The songs revealed an increased perception and breadth of vision, a growth in understanding as well as simply musical proficiency, and yet the band avoided the fatal trap of aimless musical indulgence. The need for the three minute cut off point in rock and roll was not something that they were about to ignore.

Immediacy, imagination and energy are the key factors that separate rock and roll from muzak. But on this album, The Jam were braving labels – 'rock opera', 'concept album' – which have marked other bands as pretentious. Yet The Jam succeeded.

The album opens with a nicely ironic song about the failure of understanding, with Weller bemoaning the fact that the *Girl On The Phone* is forever ringing him back. It's really a song about the failure of two people to communicate on any level other than that dictated by convention; the girl's feelings are not reciprocated, but she cannot accept that. To her boy/girl relationships are always of one specific type, with the female in a position of admiration, and she adopts that position because she's been conditioned to accept it.

And yet the song is something more than that. The girl knows everything about the object of her infatuation even though they have never met. She knows:

'Where I get my trousers, where I get my socks,
My leg measurements and the size of my cock'

Every little detail is known, but they're all *physical* details, and in that respect the song shows how Weller has become conscious of the fact that the only real communication springs from within. It's something more than simple physical contact that people should be seeking.

It's an idea which finds extension on *Thick As Thieves*, the first of four songs central to the primary theme of the album. That theme was based around the attitudes of three characters who, having once been old friends, find their ideals and values moving in vastly different directions as they grow older. The characters grew out of a fictional situation planned by Weller and Dave Waller as the possible basis for a book. Each of them is meant to have adopted a specific outlook on life–one becoming left-wing, one moving to the right, whilst the third, the character closest to Weller himself, takes some sort of uncommited middle road. What the four songs concerned are meant to show are the different points of view of each of the characters, whilst, as in much of his previous writing, Weller leaves the final judgement up to the listener.

Thick As Thieves is the introduction, and it details very movingly the growth of a perfect relationship in which nothing comes between the two friends and their enjoyment of life. There were no 'personal situations' to impede the relationship and the picture that is painted is unashamedly idealistic in nature, almost fairy-taleish:

'We stole the burning sun in the open sky,
We stole the twinkling stars in the black night,
We stole the green-belt fields that made us believe,
We stole everything that we could see'

Perhaps it's this kind of relationship that Weller is personally seeking, although he knows that it's an impossible one to carry through. Age brings with it a rigidity and inability to understand, and the pressures of life slowly erode the essential nature of idealism.

Yet often it's not a gradual process–if it were, it might be possible

94

to guard against it–in some cases it's almost instantaneous:

> 'But something came along that changed our minds,
> I don't know what and I don't know why,
> But we grew up in a flash of time,
> As we watched our ideals helplessly unwind'

Thick As Thieves shares with the earlier Away From The Numbers the same direct insight into Weller's emotions that are only hinted at in the rest of his writing.

It's primarily a very romantic song, one that's passionate, arousing and directly fulfilling without being simply twee. Whereas in the past, notably on The Modern World, the band's music had perhaps fallen short of the target, this one was a direct hit.

The next song on the album, Private Hell, concerns itself with the archetypal frustrated housewife, but the treatment that the subject is given avoids merely restating old clichés and platitudes. It deals once again with the death of the individual, with the frustration at having opportunities denied and with the pain of finding that even those who are meant to be closest are quite unable to understand:

> 'Think of Edward, still at college,
> You send him letters
>   that he doesn't acknowledge,
> 'Cause he don't care, they don't care'

Everyone is locked inside their own little box, and because of that communication is denied. Modern society, by its very nature, denies people their humanity, and the death of the individual becomes inevitable. Yet once again The Jam cannot offer any real solution; the final line of Sanity At last inside your own Private Hell states simply that, in the present scheme of things, the only way to cope with life is to shrink away from it and to deny your own potential for growth.

The elitism that twentieth century society breeds, whether capitalist or communist, is something that The Jam find impossible to understand, and the consequences of it are clearly outlined in Little Boy Soldiers. No-one has any time for the ordinary man in the street until there's a war to be fought, and those in power see the whole thing as a matter of figures and hypothetical casualties rather than in terms of human beings. Again it's a return to the theme of the denial of man's humanity, and it shows Weller finding it harder and harder to accept the world of injustice in which he finds himself.

There's a constant sense of him feeling that he simply doesn't belong and he's searching not only for an identity but also for a home. It's reminiscent of Lennon's plight in the late '60's, and the two of them bear comparison because, like Lennon, Weller doesn't feel particularly special. Sure he's a fine musician and idol of millions, but essentially he feels just as much a man in the street as the kids who come to see The Jam.

The message of *Little Boy Soldiers* is that the whole rigmarole of fighting 'Beneath the flag of democracy' for a 'better world' is a sham. All that's important to the average kid is whether he's got enough money for a pint. Wars don't mean a thing, neither do doctrines or ideologies, and what matters most is whether there's enough to eat and a place to sleep.

It's a technically ambitious song, its rhythm changes and separate sections reminiscent of *Strange Town*, whilst the middle-eight sounds very Sid Barrett-ish, and once again the band showed themselves pushing to present things in a new and interesting fashion. The acoustic interlude, with Weller singing:

'Sit right down, I'll sing you a lullaby,
And tell you a tale of how goodness prevailed,
We killed and robbed, the fucking lot'

has the same discomforting quality that characterises the Floyd's early, and best, work.

The song which is probably the most accurate barometer of the mood of the album is *Wasteland*, with its bleak language and stark symbolism, and together with *Saturday's Kids* it reveals much of The Jam's collective attitude to life. The latter is basically a reiteration of *Mr. Clean*, but this time the problem is placed right in the forefront:

'It's the system, hate the system,
WHAT'S THE SYSTEM?'

It all appears very clichéd but these Saturday's Kids are real people, the 'life blood of the nation', and yet they're channelled and marketed like so many cattle. It's this kind of injustice that The Jam concern themselves with:

'There's more reason to write about real life than there is in birds, flowers or whatever. I've not got the answers and I don't want to claim to either. The ones who try and solve the world's problems always get killed off–Jesus, Che Guevara, Martin Luther King.... I'm waiting for the answers as well.'

Wasteland is the second song in the quartet about the three characters, and it portrays the immediate aftermath of the destruction of a friendship. The loss of the innocence and romance of youth, the idealism that Weller finds so appealing, is lost, leaving only desolation and despair:

> 'To be caught smiling is to acknowledge life,
> A brave but useless show of compassion,
> And that is forbidden in this
>   drab and colourless world'

The relationship has been irrevocably destroyed and the survivors are left to seek their own escape. How they do so depends upon their own inclinations, but the right-wing individual of the three states his case in *Burning Sky*.

The song takes the form of a letter, an unusual and ambitious construction:

> 'But work comes first, I'm sure you'll understand...
> There's no time for dreams when commerce calls'

One escape from the system is to buy your way out, to work so hard as a cog in the machinery that ultimately you can remove yourself and set yourself up in your own little world. It's one point of view–and The Jam display it as disinterestedly as they can–and whether you agree with it or not is left up to you. The Jam obviously don't.

That doesn't mean to say that they're averse to making money: 'I found at one time that I couldn't care less, didn't give a monkey's about whether I was earning a lot or a little, but now the more I get, the more I want.'

Yet when Weller says that there's no sense of the rich capitalist seeking greater profits. The Jam want more money to use creatively and constructively, to expand Riot Stories and to help other bands like The Vapors. What is clear is that, whatever the *Burning Sky* may mean to the character in the song, it doesn't mean the same to The Jam.

98

Also included on the album was *Smithers-Jones*, this time given a novel string arrangement. Once again, however, it was purely a one off. A matter of experimenting with various musical possibilites, and there aren't going to be any Jam orchestral albums in the future.

What was interesting about the song was that, taking the same type of character as *Mr. Clean*, it conveyed an entirely different meaning. There's a sense of compassion and understanding, and it showed The Jam extending their scope of interest beyond the limits of the earlier songs. It's an understanding of the plight of people as a whole rather than simply kids, and Foxton's lyrics reveal a sense of empathy with the middle-aged commuter. Again, barriers are transcended and deeper communication sought.

The last verse of the song was in fact a contribution from Weller, and the final couplet sums up his perception of the world:

'Work and work and work till you die,
There's plenty more fish in the sea to fry'

The cannon fodder of *Little Boy Soldiers* are seen to be no less exploited in ordinary society.

The final track of the quartet is *Eton Rifles*, a jolly sing-song which also proved to be one of their most successful singles. The character under discussion is the left winger, but the song as a whole is meant as an indictment of the fact that in the 1980's there still exists a clearly observable class system–something Weller finds not only distasteful but also quite unbelievable. Public school cadets playing with rifles and uniforms seem quite ridiculous in a civilised society, and the perpetuation of an elite in this wealth-dominated system is very disturbing, but The Jam aren't so naïve as to think that the situation's going to be changed by hip left wing platitudes. Too many 'revolutionaries' are only after a little excitement or even power for themselves, playing trendy left wing games whilst perpetuating the very system they claim to dislike:

'You composed a revolutionary symphony,
Then went to bed with a charming young thing'

All they can offer is the alternative rock and roll has always offered–to dance on your problems. The inclusion on the album of *Heatwave*, the almost obligatory '60's track, emphasised that first and foremost, rock and roll is for dancing to.

Despite the critical and commercial success of the album, and its obvious musical accomplishment, the band weren't completely satisfied. Less than half the songs – namely the quartet concerning the central theme – were considered totally successful.

Nonetheless, Weller's lyrics were gifted, subtle and often highly perceptive comments on contemporary values and lifestyles. Primarily, the album set out to examine England and its history, its people and its possible future, and in that respect it was archetypal Jam. The seemingly inevitable destruction of not only the individual, but also communities and relationships, came under scrutiny and the band proved themselves well able to extend their musical horizons:

'We're getting more and more into rhythm, like African drum music and things like that.'

The need to have an evolving musical style is something of which the band are acutely aware, but it's not always a conscious evolution – it's only with the benefit of hindsight that the innovation of *Strange Town* and *Little Boy Soldiers* can be perceived – but it is a process which depends upon the band as a whole.

Foxton and Buckler are as involved in the production of the music as is Weller, and they give the latter's sometimes disparate ideas a definite shape and sound. Without their contribution, much of the material would be far less cohesive, and within the band there's a tacit acknowledgement that they are all as important as each other.

And yet one of the inevitable consequences of the music business is that there's always someone in a band who is regarded as the leader. In The Jam it's obviously Weller who receives most of the attention – he's the spokesman, writing the vast majority of the songs, and so, to a certain extent, he moulds the philosophy and direction of the band. So while it's true that the sense of unity in the band negates Weller as some kind of dictator, he's undoubtedly regarded as the figurehead.

His material very often diagnoses various problems, always with an acute understanding of the symptoms, but he won't go in for facile solutions. He's a rock and roll singer and he knows it; he's not a politician. What he seems most concerned with is finding a way in which he can function on his own terms, with a few compromises and as little disharmony as possible.

The Jam's songs are mini-chronicles, recording contemporary situations and events. The characters are people you could meet in any pub, in any street–*Billy Hunt* and *Mr. Clean*, the guys in *Eton Rifles* and *Burning Sky*, are just opposite ends of the same spectrum, individuals finding that such a chasm exists, between them that communication seems impossible. It's that communication which The Jam are trying to provoke, taking as their targets the claustrophobia and inhibition of modern society, the limited expectations and opportunities that people have–but they don't react unthinkingly. Weller's described himself as 'possibly an armchair radical', but what he does believe is that it's the determination of people within themselves to remain unaffected that matters. He knows that politics and 'revolution' change nothing, that there's always someone who wants to be a new Hitler or Ayatollah, and that the same problems will surface again. *Eton Rifles* satirizes all the trendy left wing intellectuals who are into 'social change' and 'people's rights' simply because it's the fashion. Next year they may well be fascists, so who's the enemy?

Weller might seem to avoid responsibility, but by doing so he leaves the decision in your hands. He sometimes inhibits the expressions of his feelings because he knows that he just doesn't have the answers yet. He's astute enough to realise that what he feels today he may well reject tomorrow, and the sense of impermanence he feels in life leads him to direct the whole of his energies into what he's doing at the minute.

He sees things very much in terms of tribal existence, with people living in cliques and groups outside of which they don't seem able to function. The only possible link he can provide between them all is music–and that's what he uses. In the meantime, he's found that the greatest focus of his attention has been the essential Englishness of this country, and perhaps because of that The Jam have found America a tough nut to crack. It's not something that they're unduly worried about, however; they're happy to be English, and if the U.S. wants them, it can have them–but only on their terms.

March 1980 saw the release of *Going Underground* which, with the advance orders of well over two hundred thousand, shot straight into the charts at number one–the first time that's happened for seven years. It was a well-crafted little rocker which reiterated The Jam's dissatisfaction with the world:

 'The public gets what the public wants,
  But I want nothing this society's got'

Perhaps the best single of the year, it rightly met with much critical favour and showed Weller at his most fiercely dismissive. *Going Underground* showed The Jam as having mastered their chosen art form and Paul Weller in particular as having gained a confidence that no longer fed on mere arrogance. They were touring the US when news came of the enormous success of *Going Underground* and the band came back to give two celebratory gigs at the late-lamented Rainbow in Finsbury Park. It was here that Mick Talbot joined the band, augmenting the Jam's spare live sound with keyboards. It should have sounded alarm bells—in two years' time Mick Talbot would join Weller to form Style Council.

The band found themselves in a secure position: they had arrived at last. The *New Musical Express* Poll for 1979 saw The Jam win practically every section open to them, and despite the obvious satisfaction, their response summed up their future course: 'It's great to gain recognition—but then we always knew how good we were. What we want to see next year is someone challenging us for the top places. Music's got to improve, got to evolve to be worthwhile.'

The second half of 1980 saw The Jam forging ahead with their usual determination. Weller's interest in the music of the sixties encouraged him to buy a sitar and the band set off to conquer the Far East. Japanese youth culture has always revered Western rock'n'roll and The Jam were received with the sort of adulation previously reserved for The Beatles. The tour of Japan was a resounding success—even spawning the infamous white vinyl bootleg, *Burning Sky*—and served to re-state their position.

1980 also saw the publication of the first issue of *December's Child*, the magazine brought out by Weller's newly-formed publishing company, Riot Stories. It was intended to be a vehicle through which the talents of various poets, writers and artists could be given a public showing. The standard was variable, but at least Weller was trying to give unknown artists and writers the chance to prove themselves.

However in other ways the band was becoming less accessible. Fans were no longer let in to sound checks as a matter of course; recording became a private affair. While practicalities probably made this inevitable, there were criticisms made that The Jam no longer practised what they preached. They appeared to be drawing

102

away from the hectic world that had previously been a source of much needed stimulation.

However it didn't stop them touring, and for the time being it didn't stop them recording either. Touring America (without much impact), Finland and Denmark, they began trying out new material. It became apparent that Weller was widening his sphere of interest and the single released in November 1980–originally entitled *Two Minutes*, but later re-titled *Start!*, was not a disappointment. With stinging rhythm guitar and pulsing bass sound, it was a song to dance to–pop with a capital P. The record went in to the BBC charts at Number 3, and maintained The Jam's popularity over the winter season. They had been touring the UK since September, helping local bands by bringing them in to open for them in the third slot at each venue. It was a simple gesture, and didn't cost The Jam anything, but no-one else was doing it.

While the tour progressed fans waited for the new album, and

divided into two lines of thought – either The Jam were as good as they'd ever been and would get better, or they were showing signs of weakness and it would be wise to delay judgement. The release of *Sound Affects* did nothing to reconcile these two strands.

Sound Affects was the point at which Paul Weller thought the band peaked. It was, he said later, "a fuckin' classic LP. I thought there was something that was *really, really* good there." He acknowledged his debt to George Orwell, a writer he admired, in spite of being "a public school boy". *Homage to Catalonia* was a seminal book for Paul Weller; he believed that Orwell's description of the utopian socialist society of Barcelona early in the Spanish Civil War showed that there could be a better, non-elitist way to run society. Yet the very success of *Sound Affects*, and of *Going Underground* which he later dismissed as trite, probably encouraged the rot to set in as far as Weller was concerned.

Sound Affects was clearly Weller's attempt to re-write *Revolver*, and in that way was partly successful. There were numerous good tracks, nearly all of them instantly appealing, but then again, so is a choc ice. One of the more immediate impressions was that it was a brighter, cleaner sound than they had made use of in *Setting Sons*. But it seemed to indicate a quest for a new sound – a looking back which didn't augur well for the future.

Sound Affects saw a conscious attempt on Weller's part to make his writing that much more succinct, to get the message over in as few words as possible, but he seems to have overdone this at times, with some of the lyrics almost too symbolic. It all raised an interesting but worrying question – whether The Jam had burned themselves out on *Setting Sons* in terms of sustained attacks on targets of social injustice.

Depending on your point of view, *Sound Affects* showed The Jam as having mastered their art, or was a disappointment and indicated that things were not quite as wonderful as they might have been. Of eleven tracks, perhaps only *Pretty Green, Monday, Man In The Corner Shop* and *That's Entertainment* (released as a single by the German record company and imported into the UK) really impressed. The Jam looked a little too much like they were treading water, but things weren't so terrible that there was no hope of recovery.

The rest of the band, its management, and especially the music

press and the fans, continued to feel that The Jam was on an upward curve. The band scooped the pool in just about every end of year poll or award at the end of 1980 but at the *Daily Mirror* Rock and Pop Awards, Paul mortified everyone by refusing to go up and receive the award for Best Single. Bruce Foxton and Rick Buckler went up on their own, feeling utterly humiliated. But for Paul it was a stand against what he most disliked about the music business–and with some justification, as the others picked up the award to the strain of a massed brass band playing *Going Underground*. It's just that he hadn't warned the others. Or consulted them. And this was to be the pattern for the next two years.

The band members were beginning to lead separate lives. The laddish drunken antics which had habitually peppered their tours became less frequent; Paul began to bring his girlfriend Gill along. Bruce and Rick's girlfriends would occasionally join them on tour, but didn't much enjoy it–so when Gill was with Paul the others were thrown on each other's company and the trio inevitably grew apart. Paul kept his cards close to his chest, and the others–apparently even John Weller–did not really know what he was thinking and planning.

There was a hiatus in 1981. The pressure to produce an album was off, and it provided a time for reflection, although the non-stop touring continued. Once again they failed to break in the States. And it must be said that one reason for their comparative failure there lay in their own hands. The uncompromising attitude that has always been essential to the band maybe didn't wash with the hip young executives in the land of the free–their absolute self-assurance probably worked against them there.

As the year progressed it became apparent that critically everything was not sweetness and light in the UK either. Concert reviews became less ecstatic and impatience was building over the delay in releasing new material. They did make a couple of singles–*Funeral Pyre* and *Absolute Beginners*. At the end of 1980, they took on a new producer, Peter Wilson, who had been a Polygram engineer. In practice, this meant Paul Weller was controlling the change of sound. However *Funeral Pyre* was not well-received–it was shrouded in a sticky, unwholesome sound and didn't sell well.

The release date of a new album was put off until March 1982, but the release of *Absolute Beginners* helped to whet the appetite of

106

anxious fans, as unlike *Funeral Pyre*, it appeared to show The Jam pushing forward in new directions. However it didn't do well by The Jam's standards, and didn't get much radio play either.

In the summer of 1981 Lady Diana Spencer was married to the Prince of Wales in front of a worldwide live television audience of hundreds of millions. In the same summer race riots broke out in Brixton and Liverpool. The juxtaposition of haves and have-nots was not lost on Weller. But he also didn't believe that rock'n'roll music could change things politically; he was scathing about the *New Musical Express* which he believed personified the false search for the radicalisation of the young through rock. Rock music had no power, he said later, "It's totally redundant. It's just a big fucking vehicle for nothing. It's like the Emperor's new clothes, it's got nothing at all." But he did channel some of his political frustration into the Campaign for Nuclear Disarmament, becoming a member, and declaring it "the only positive political movement at the moment". At the end of 1981 the band gave four CND benefit gigs and contributed a track (*Little Boy Soldier*) to a CND compilation. But at the turn of the year, unknown to anyone else, Paul had already begun to think about calling it a day with The Jam.

This was in spite of opening 1982 with another Number 1 single, *A Town Called Malice*. Its music was Motown-inspired, but the words were strictly UK early-eighties recession-inspired:

> *Cut down on beer or the kids new gear*
> *It's a big decision in a town called Malice.*

This single was contained in their next and sixth album, called *The Gift*. And as far as the listening public was concerned, it was a gift. It showed The Jam fighting for something slightly different–less antagonistic and more positive. The lyrics showed Weller consciously trying to re-affirm his position, his identification with the man in the street, while all the time he was conscious that other people wanted to place him continually on some kind of artificial pedestal. The positive stance that seemed to be characterising the band's work more and more was epitomised in the line from *A Town Called Malice* where Weller sings of how he'd prefer to restore joy to people's lives than simply document the iniquities of the situation as it stands.

107

To many fans *The Gift* was the band's most complete, cohesive album to date. It was ironic because ultimately, Paul Weller was not satisfied with the end result. Even though he had had a year out from the pressure of annual album production, he felt stifled by the idea of churning out albums year in, year out: "It was the thought of the next ten years, keep doing that for the next ten years. I just wanted to get off the roundabout for a while." Rick and Bruce's reaction to the album was understandably more upbeat. "We thought we'd done a good job on the album," they said in their 1993 book, *The Jam: Our Story*. "Obviously Paul was heading off in a new direction, but there was nothing that he was writing then or subsequently that we didn't think we could have turned our hand to."

But that didn't enter the equation with Paul Weller. He wanted out, and he wanted to quit while they were on top. By the time

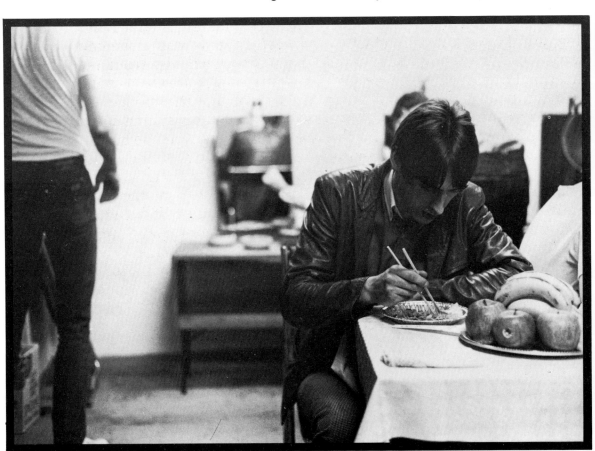

their 1982 summer single, *The Bitterest Pill*, was released, Paul had already delivered the bombshell – he was leaving The Jam, closing it down, getting out. He would honour their commitments to the end of the year, with a real farewell tour for all the fans, and that would be it. He had made the decision while on holiday with Gill in Italy, and had not even consulted his father, John.

The Jam's demise was probably one of the worst kept secrets in the history of rock. Rumours began to circulate in the late summer and early autumn, and although Weller had planned to make the official announcement during their appearance on Channel 4's 'The Tube' in November, things had got to such a pitch that a hurried statement was released to the media at the end of October. This was probably to the viewers' advantage: The Jam's 'Tube' special remains one of the all-time great live TV sessions, perhaps because the prior announcement of the split enabled them to relax into the music.

Weller provided an exclusive interview to his friend Paolo Hewitt in *Melody Maker*, in which he outlined his reasons. "If we had carried on, the whole thing would have dissipated just from the sheer fact of carrying on," he said. He wanted to be taken seriously as a writer, but didn't just want to carry on for the money. He claimed to want to "get back to just sitting down and writing songs because I enjoy it, not because I've got any standards to live up to." But he also let slip a more personal reason – and it was to do with getting older. In both this sympathetic interview and a more rebarbative one in the *New Musical Express* at the end of the year, Weller revealed an acute embarrassment at the idea of being an ageing rock star, still pumping out the same material twenty years on. "I don't like the thought of imagining The Jam when we're 30 and old and embarrassing," he confided. He was 24 years old at the time. "I don't know how some of these old groups have got the gall to do it; to go out there. They must either be stupid or really don't care. I couldn't do it. I couldn't look people in the face."

Weller was asked at the time whether Bruce and Rick thought the same way as him about the close-down of The Jam. "I think so, yeah. I think they do. I'm probably a bit more dogmatic," Weller said, "but I still think they do believe in it actually." He conceded that they were "a bit shocked, really, but I think after a while they'll see what I'm saying is right." The problem was, no-one

actually asked their opinion, least of all Weller. The farewell tour, ending with a series of gigs at Wembley, was not particularly happy. Fans showed their resentment, pressing backstage to demand a reason for the split–a question that Bruce and Rick couldn't really answer. "We felt a lot of bitterness," they said later. "Having worked so hard for so many years to achieve this level of popularity, we didn't really want to throw in the towel at the height of our careers. Not just the five years we had been professional, but for five years before that we had been more than just a band. For us Paul's decision didn't add up at all."

When the split was announced, The Jam's label, Polydor, released all their singles at once, so that the band had thirteen in the Top 100 at the same time. Paul Weller moved on quickly–too quickly for the others' comfort–to form Style Council in which he tried to pursue his dream of producing a distinct English soul sound. The Jam's records continue to sell in huge numbers throughout the world, as each succeeding year a new group of adolescents identifies with the sentiments of *Trans-global Express*, *Eton Rifles* and *Going Underground*. Weller has now gone solo, having passed the thirty-year-old watershed without mishap. Foxton and Buckler have come to terms with the past. And in the end, Paul Weller was right–The Jam was the personification of an age and a time, and their youthful, exuberant, yet angry pop tunes endure on that basis.